LET'S TALK ABOUT IT.

Braedon Bell

It is estimated that more than 350 million people worldwide suffer from a form of depression, which is more than 5% of the Earth's population.

Bipolar disorder affects around 60 million people.

Schizophrenia affects an estimated 21 million people worldwide.

Anorexia Nervosa, Bulimia Nervosa, and other eating disorders affect around 70 million people each year.

Nearly 1 million people with mental disorders commit suicide every single year. Many of these are teenagers.

There are 297 disorders in the DSM -IV. If so many people are experiencing this, why is it so unapproachable? So stigmatized?

Only 41% of adults in the U.S. with a mental health conditions received the needed treatment and/or services within the past year.
Through donating a percentage of the proceeds of this book to mental health organizations, I hope we can improve that statistic.

In my short 20 years, by
December of 2017, I had been deeply
affected by a series of tragic events.
These events instilled in me a desire to
try to make a difference in the area of
mental health. I wanted to come together
with a community of people to create
something unique - not just poetry but
unity and awareness. I started by creating
an Instagram page in order to promote
Mental Health Awareness. I posted a few
thoughts about what I was hoping to
achieve. Through this, I reached a larger
audience than I had anticipated. My inbox
was immediately filled with messages from
people ready to help me reach my goal. I
had conversations with them about their
lives and daily struggles. I realized that
many of them were just trying to make it
through their
minutes/hours/days/weeks/months/years. My
goal is that this book will open your eyes
to the seriousness of having a mental
disorder. I hope that you can relate to
some of these struggles and sympathize
with the writers.

Society is either apathetic, or has
created an enormous stigma attached to
having a mental disorder. Unfortunately,
many times it is too late by the time
others around the individual understand
the extent of their sadness or challenge.
It is my goal to hopefully shed a small
light on this, hoping one day to destroy
this stigma, raise
awareness, and create a support system for
people struggling with mental disorders.

We live in a society that is accepting of
injuries of most all areas of the body,
except one of most importance - our minds
- the single entity that keeps our bodies
functioning and our hope alive.

Let's talk about it.

Braedon Bell

ACKNOWLEDGMENTS

It's very difficult to open up to a stranger. Therefore I want to express my deepest appreciation to all of the writers who contributed and shared their stories with me. Thank you to my mother, Betina Bell, for being able to convert feelings and poems into the powerful illustrations pictured in this book. Thank you to all of my friends and family for supporting me along this journey and thank you, the reader, for joining us in this campaign to create a safer, more aware environment for those who struggle with mental health.

Together we can change the world.

Some authors chose to share their names
with you, while others wished to remain
anonymous. It is my hope that one day
those who are apprehensive to speak out
will no longer remain silent.

DEDICATION

This book is dedicated to Abby, a sister
and a friend who I wish I could have
gotten to know better, and to the many
families and friends who have lost loved
ones struggling with these disorders.

Before you continue, please note that you
are encountering potentially graphic
material and that the images expressed in
these pages are conveying experiences,
which are subjective to the writer.

I am not a possible person, place or
thing.
I am a human
I am not a fact or a statistic
I am not to be used as an adjective
I am not being "OCD" as I use exactly
4 grains of sugar with my tea in the
morning
I am not acting depressed like it's a
show on Broadway
I am not feeling down
I am not crazy
I am not flawed
I am not
I am not
I am not

I am human.

                    - anonymous

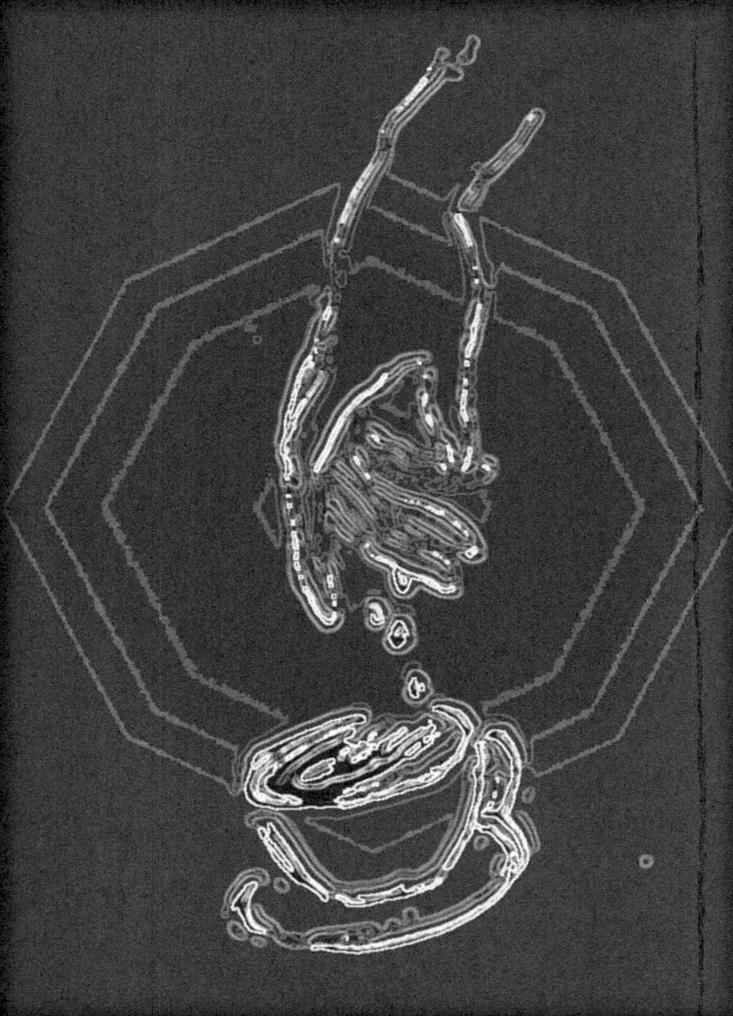

I'm not crazy
I want to scream
Why do people say these things?
I am just a girl with an issue or two
If you could just understand the
things I have to go through
I'm just me,
As you are you
But if you could only hear the things
I have to go through
No, I'm not talking about my disorder
Although that's hard too
I'm talking about the whispers
The quiet voices of judgment and hate
that make me feel unworthy and not at
all great
If you only knew what all I have to go
through
Maybe the stigma would stop spreading
too
People would reach out and start
seeing
People would understand why sometimes
it's hard for me to keep breathing
My mind fights against me you see
It may look like I'm fine but it's all
a delusion
I live a double life that acts as my
illusion

                    - anonymous

I started a garden when I was 8
At first, beautiful flowers grew
Daisies, roses, and tulips of every
color
One day when I walked outside
All the flowers were dead except one
This one was small and fragile
I focused all my time on making sure
it was okay
I watered only that flower and never
tried to grow any others again
Sometimes I would go outside and be so
proud of my flower
Some days it would grow just enough to
make me think one day maybe it would
bloom and I could start gardening
again
The winter came and I moved it into a
greenhouse so it would never feel cold
again
Although now I am feeling cold
I'm 20 now and just now realizing
That my flower never bloomed
Despite all my efforts
I spent 12 years focused on something
that never gave anything in return
I went to my now empty garden
I went to my flower
This flower wasn't actually a flower
at all
This flower was a weed
This weed had suffocated the rest of
my garden and never allowed me to
replant
This weed was called depression

They don't know how hard it is

They don't know that somedays my sheets
wrap around my neck so tightly that I
can't move

They only see me on the days that I manage
to loosen myself from their grip, pick up
my feet and force them to move just so I
can be normal. They call this *waking up.*

They don't know how hard it is for me to
go to a place where 50 other people are
eager to make conversation in coherence to
filling their bodies with alcohol while my
body is filling its insides with anxiety
and fear. They only hear the words that
manage to regurgitate out of my mouth just
so they don't think I'm unfriendly. *They
call this going out.*

They don't know how hard it is for me to
go through everyday wondering why I am not
like everyone else. Growing physically and
mentally at the same rate as the average
person yet feeling so behind and alone.

I'm the kind of sick that you don't see.

I'm the kind of sick that doesn't get
better

So I pick myself up and keep going so I
can be normal. They call this *life.*

- anonymous

.. feel crazy all of the time"

"even to feel crazy is to feel anything at
all"

                    -   anonymous

Someone once told me - the way I live is a

   harmony. They told me their life was a

song, but I am nothing like a song. I am a

storm. I am a force of nature, I twist and

   turn and scream like wind when I'm mad.

I'm full of passion and my lightening can

  be seen from miles away. I am fierce and

   when my rain pours you could be drowned.

With that being said, I reach the flowers

   whose stems have been crushed and I fill

their roots with hope. I nourish the life

with fuel-the growth around and within me.

I am here, because like everything, the

earth needs balance. There are girls who

   are songs. I am a storm.

                              - anonymous

Sometimes it gets so hard. My body feels
like concrete and the effort of having to
pick myself up feels like I'm swimming
with anchors on my feet.

I'm sinking

I'm drowning…

- anonymous

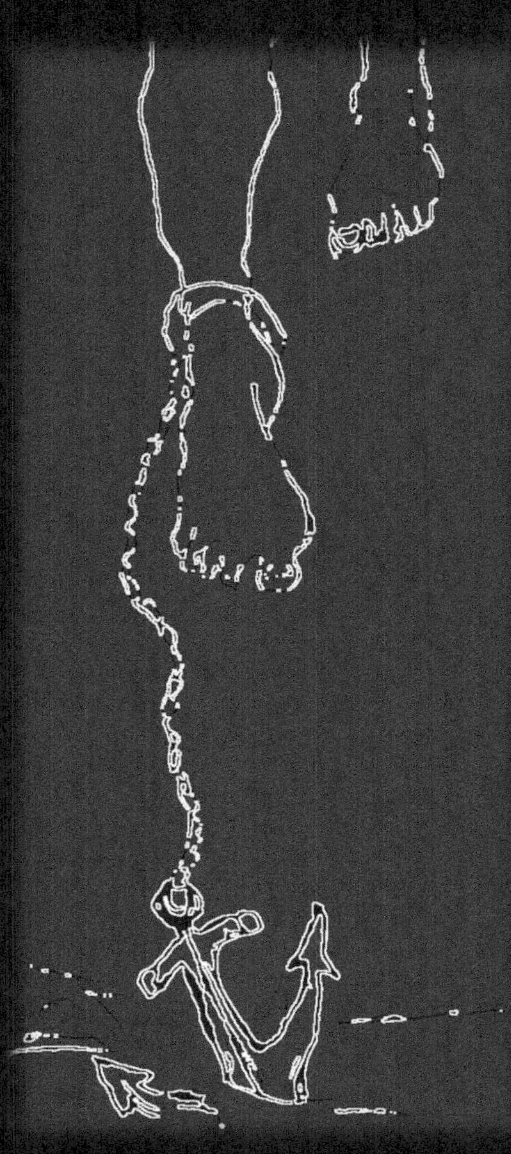

They rip holes in our jeans and charge
$130 a pair

They distress sweaters for 60 dollars

I was born with a hole in my heart and
distress in my mind, and they charge me a
small monthly fee of $49.99 for anti-
depressants and $60.00 a session

Retail

-    anonymous

Why must things be this way, I hate
going through this day by day.

Constant hands gripping my feet,

I want to fly but they tell me to
sink.

                    - anonymous

What is poetry?

Are the sad people attracted to poetry or is
poetry attracted to sad people

Or are we in love

Or did we just fall out of love

Or are we just sad and we like being sad

Why is poetry often sad

Is it because we are often sad?

                    -    anonymous

I once wrote a diary full of words
Words of love and hurt

All my secrets and darkest fears

Then I shredded it into a fine dust

and used it as sugar for my coffee

                        -   anonymous

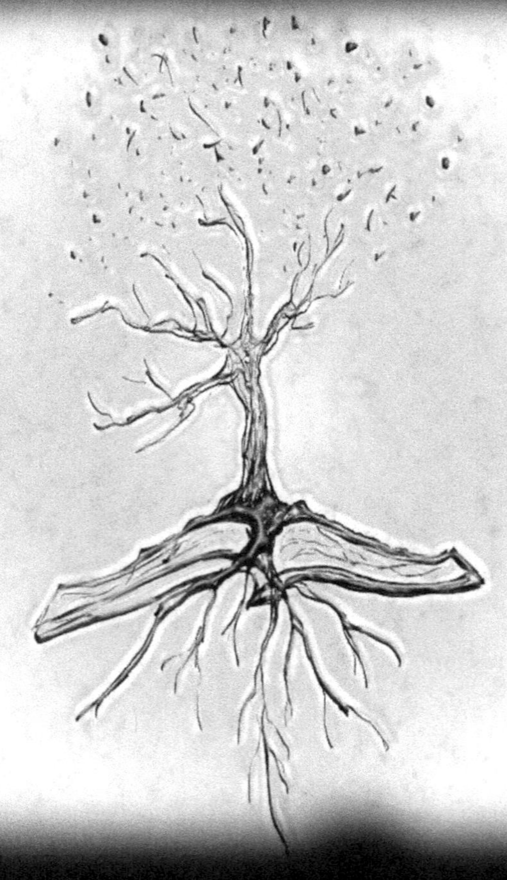

I always thought I was born to be a
mother

I thought the one thing I was sure of was

that I wanted to procreate

It is an innate biological need, is it
not?

Then I started thinking

What if my child felt like me

What if I passed on these twisted flawed
genes of sadness and pain

If I can't take care of me how would I
take care of another

cats are easy to care for

So now I think

Maybe I'll get a cat

- anonymous

They say once you become addicted to
something you will never be the same
Which makes me think
What really makes us change?
I would say that I was addicted to you
I would say you were addicted to
things too
                         We were both addicted
                    both changing, growing
     you became dependent on substances to
                         make you feel new
      I relied on what I thought I knew to
                                  be true

So does this make us different?

        Or are we the same?

                Both exchanging
     pleasure for pain.

                  - anonymous

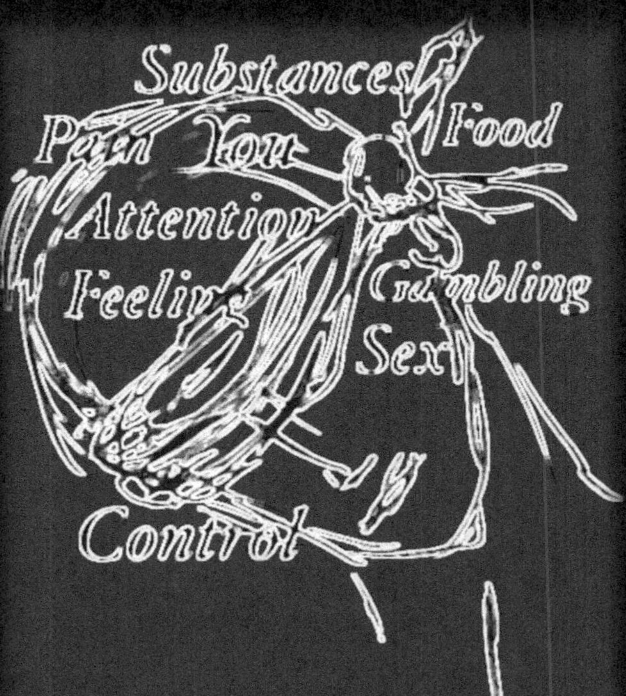

Substances
Pain
You
Food
Attention
Feeling
Gambling
Sex
Control

You seem like a shell of what used to be
I look at you,
searching an entity
You act like this earth will
fall
     off
          its
               axle
I hate seeing you look so fragile
I look again

Shadows of dreams that were crushed
Echoes of doors that closed
You were once so full of life
now it looks like someone
scraped the last of your hope
out with a butter knife

                    - anonymous

Humans are amazing.

We are creatures that live to be noticed,
and then scream for peace.

We are each unique

We act different

We are different

So why treat us all the same?

We need to be rewarded for our differences
not punished.

I want to be seen as a equal yes but also
as an individual.

I am weird

stubborn

difficult

amazing.

I am different

I am me.

There's just a glitch in my system

I try to explain

It's hard for me not to feel pain

I try for sunshine

And only find rain

It's not every day I feel this way

Somedays I'm fine and full of light

Others I'm wandering in constant night

It's not too bad you must know

Because everything that dies

Once had a chance to grow

- anonymous

You are innocent and beautiful. You
are struggling. But I'm here. This is
not your fault. You are going to get
through this and I'm going to help
you.

-things I wish I could have said

                    - anonymous

Storming into my room,

I just wanted to get away,

The thoughts that possessed me,

Stayed in my head all day.

Betrayal, anger, and even hate,

Always there and never gone,

I wasn't thinking

It was too late

No one could stop me, it had to be done.

I went to school in the morning,

These emotions here again,

I was in the corridor, just walking

Being pushed and shoved and hit,

I just wanted to escape,

This horror of a world I lived in,

I couldn't cope anymore,

Taking shape, I lay down and left

My mother found me,

She rang the ambulance,

And they arrived shortly

After, saving me,

But I didn't want saving.

                        -   anonymous

You've been there, you kept quiet, you
didn't argue, you bit ur tongue just
not step on their toes, you've lied
about what you really like and don't
like to get their approval but ended
up doing what you really want in guilt
and doubt.

They managed to distort your self
image and self worth, they tricked you
into believing what they're offering
is all that really is! And all what
you have is all what you can do!

You've killed yourself inside plenty
of times just to pass another night,
you've fantasized the end more than
what it could've been.

Only when you're at the rock bottom
you'll realize how beautiful and
worthwhile you are for just being able
to experience these feelings. For
being alive enough to feel this death
inside you.

                    - Oudetta

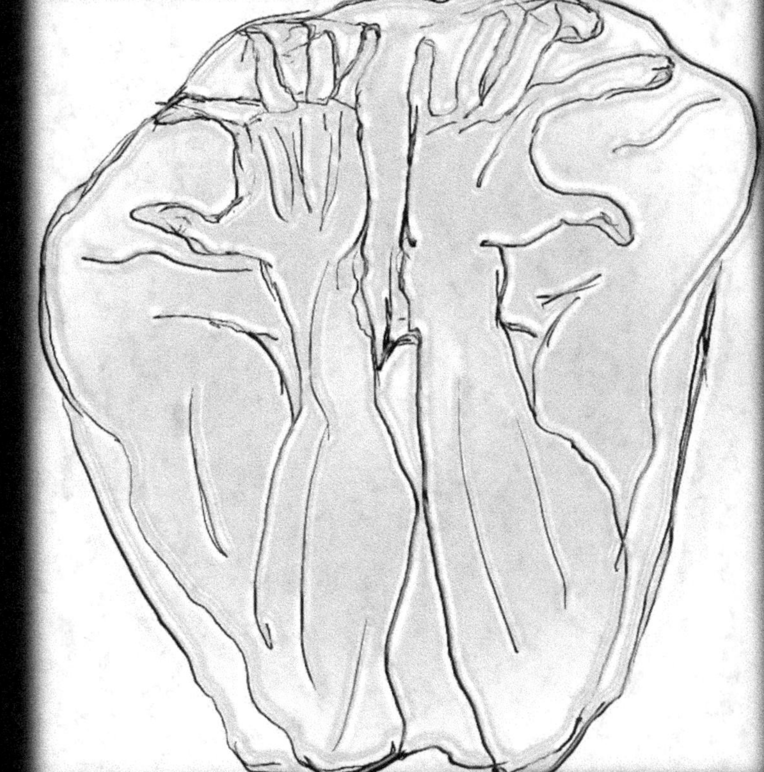

you will rise from the hurt, you will
overcome this.

        Yes, I'm talking to you.

 too bad I know that's a broken dream that
           will now never come true

                    -   anonymous

Yesterday:

I'm fighting off a dark stress cloud,

Shadow the back of mind

Like a vortex it plunges deep into the
brain,

Devouring logic, rationality and sleep.

Nightmares driven by it's foul nature,
plumes

Spiraling until disorientation accelerates

Placing me firmly in the middle of it's
eye

Today:

I created the gale that blew my stress
cloud away,

Returning to bask in you warm sunshine…

With a watchful eye ever trained to the
horizon

                    -   Alex Pike

                    Poetryinlondon
                    -

Someone will always have something to say
but you are not their words. And honestly,
you're not yours either. The voices you
hear in your head are mean and harsh. You
are neither mean, nor harsh. You are
beautiful.

Tell the voices they are WRONG.

You are not fat.

You are not stupid.

You are not inferior to anyone in ANY way.

You are **STRONG**.

You are intelligent, wonderful and you are
everything you are supposed to be.

If a caterpillar

Didn't nourish itself

It would never become a
butterfly.

- anonymous

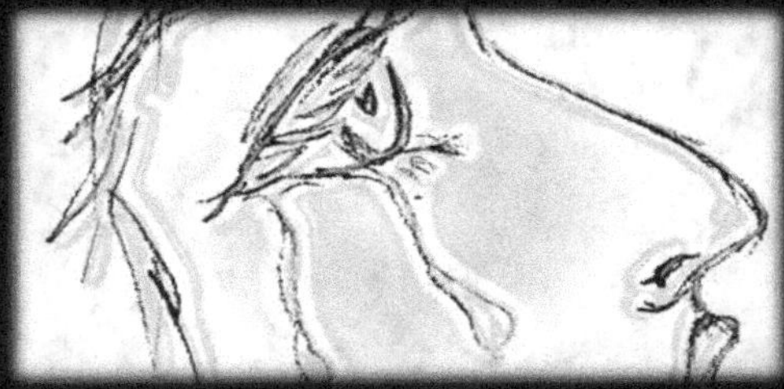

I painted my nails. I can't have food
until they dry.
Every time someone says the word carbs a
score board lights up in my brain.
You see sucking on ice cubes isn't dinner.
Being a teenager is fun isn't it?
And even though everyone thinks you can't
have a mental illness
It's difficult to talk to people because
you're constantly thinking that they have
better things to do.
It's difficult to make plans when you
can't even convince yourself to get out of
bed.
It's difficult to wait for your friends to
show up because you're worried about
people will look at you as if something is
wrong with you.
It's difficult to make conversations when
you don't have the courage to talk about
galaxies because some hotshot extrovert is
talking about a bizarre story.
I come back home and go straight to my
room lock the doors.
feels safer somehow
As if someone in my own home would try to
harm me.
I sit still and find that piece of paper
that has been scribbled on more times than
I can imagine.
This is it.

This is it
Shut up this is it.
This is
it.
I think I should stop here because
I can't tell you about the rabbit hole
without accidentally inviting you to jump
in.
I can't tell you how bad it is without it
seeming like a cry for attention

This is it.
Remove your nail paint and put a new one
on.
I can't eat until my nail paint is dry.

- Sejal Samra

The will is starving
And the breaking
Bones are starting
To show
Cold air moves
Through the lungs
Heavy
Slow
Hunger has taken on
An entirely
Different
Twist form

      - Tahreem Haq

The turmoil inside,
Wishing the anxiety would say goodbye,

Why the doubt, shame, so many names,
Fear encompassing, smothering, your very
existence,
Drowning in blackness, weakness,
shredded identity.

Leave me alone, go away, never come back,
I hate you, words said allowed with no
reply

Is there a way out?
My darling, you are the light,

- Emma S

I came to school on Tuesday
They announced such dreadful news
The student who seemed alright
Lost a battle she couldn't fight

I thought she had time
Unfortunately too much was on her
plate
I assumed she was fine
Because her appearance was seen as
great

So many questions that I ask
How come no one noticed
She came to class with a mask
She clearly wasn't focused

This simply feels unreal
That she took her life
The girl popped a pill
And used a kitchen knife

She always seemed so pleasant
Wouldn't think anything was wrong
My mind kept going to the morning
announcement
What can I say, Tuesday was too

- DnD

My name is depression,
I live all around
Maybe next door or maybe across town
I look for a victim, anyone will do
They never come to me but I come to
you.

When I take hold, I won't make a sound
When you pick yourself up, I'll push
you back down
You don't know the power, that I
possess
I only operate to cause you distress

I start off subtle, so you won't
suspect
I bide my time till I take effect
I'll strike quickly, just wait and see
There's no way you'll ever be rid of
me

I am a demon, and you are mine
The longer I stay the more I shine
I am a silent killer and damage who I
touch
Once I am here you are in my clutch

                            - Danae Brandon

What if our world was at peace and its
people were happy

What if we could live in harmony

What if we were there for people when
they needed us to be

What if everything was how it was
supposed to be

                        - anonymous

The chains have broken, I am free
There's a world of change, ahead of me
I still have fears, that I can't let go
But I paint on a smile to not let them
show

Everyone thinks I am doing so well
Maybe I am, I can't always tell
Pride is a feeling that I rarely feel
But finally, my wounds are starting to
heal

Finally, recovery is in my sight
I found the strength I needed to fight
I had to get well, I had no choice
I no longer listen to Ana's voice

                    -   Danae Brandon

"what seems to be the problem"

Tap tap tap tap tap

"nothing"

Tap tap tap tap tap tap

"are you unhappy?"

tap tap tap

"I'm fine"

Tap tap tap tap

As I carry on with this conversation

I imagine the tapping of his foot crushing
my body

Tap tap tap tap tap

I want to disappear

Tap tap tap

"I feel fine."

                    -    anonymous

When darkness descends
Blackness consumes
A shadow of pain envelopes
Hope lost and grief resumes

Constantly battling
Forgotten loss,
Your colors and light deserted
Glimmers engulfed in moss

Grasping towards beams,
Searching for hues
Treading water til' ignition
Dots of red, yellow and blues

Never stop searching
With all your might
For inevitable rainbow
That beams despite lost light

                    - Eleanor Johnson

I feel like crawling out of my skin
Wishing so hard that I could be thin
My body is something that I despise
I hate my weight, I hate my size

Pregnancy has made, my shape change
Even though my weight is in a healthy
range
I have to push through for the sake of my
child
My body is huge, my body is vile

To stay on track, that is my aim
I fake a smile to hide the pain
I need to stay strong but the outlook is
bleak
Because I am a failure and I am weak

                              - Danae Brandon

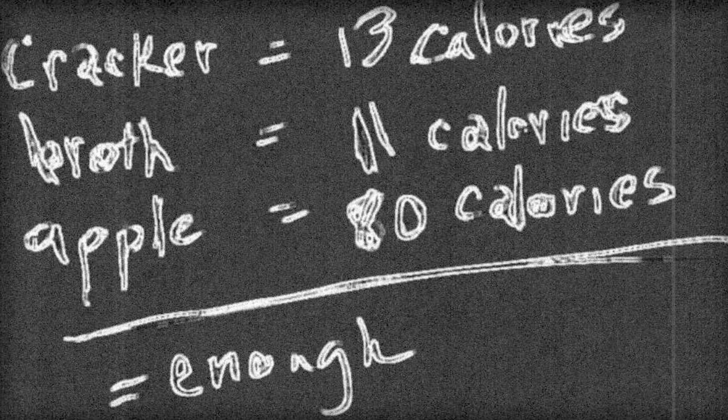

You won't always feel the crushing weight
of
The world on your shoulder- or of his body
Pressing on your chest.
I know it feels (like the sleep paralysis
he created) that no amount of
fighting will release his labored hands
from
around your shrieking waist
But you're wrong
The sacrificial blood you give to keep
your demons at bay won't continue to fall-
nor will the numbers on the scale that
falsely determine your worth as a human,
as a woman
as a daughter
as a victim
I promise you darling, you're wrong
but in all the right ways.

-   Kathryn Rowlands

Why do the medications prescribed have no
effect?
Why do I still want to break my neck?
Why do I still cut my wrists?
Why do I still take the big risks?

How is it that I'm so unstable and broken?
How is it that I'm so scarred and open?
How is it that I feel like I'm not made
for life?
And how is it I know this feelings right?

Someone once said that "life might not be
for all"
I wonder if they were talking about me,
and how far I can still fall.

When I hurt myself daily how can they let
me live my "life"?
Are they getting off, while I suffer every
night?
How do they live knowing what I do?
Tearing everything apart,
They say their worried about me,
But do they intervene?
No,
Would you?

Why don't they just stop and let me die?
They know no one can help me,
But they keep me going!
Why?
Is it so they can live?
Spending every day,
The money I give.

Is that how they keep up their lavish
life?
Taking money I don't have,
Trying to convince me that I will one day
live a "better life"?

So I keep going
Even though I want to stop,
Cutting myself up,
So they can keep a job!

One day though,
I'll be strong enough to die
to take the pills,
And not feel guilty about why!

                    -   Amy Passmore
                        Amylee16p

How can I ignore the voices,
when they're only talking to me?
How can I ignore the visions,
when I'm the only one that can see?

They tell me things that are quite
often true.
They show me things they wouldn't show
you.

I'm scared of what they'll do if I
don't listen.
I'm frightened of what will become of
me
if I don't give them attention.

                    - Amy Passmore
                      Amylee16p

Bleed

Most people I've met bleed far more black
than red
You can't see it in their tears, you can't
see it in their sweat.
You can't see it in their eyes, you can't
see it in their heads.
Most people I've met bleed far more black
than red.

Some of the black blood is hereditary,
genetic.
One day she's a luminary, seconds later
frenetic.
Just like her father, bleeds black for a
half an hour then slaps on a plaster.
But it's harder. Sometimes she can't see
where the scars are, so she gets angry and
hits
things harder and faster, black blood
drips from every crack in the wall, her
white
carpet would look like mud if anyone could
see it at all

Most people bleed far more black than red.
Some people need Prozac then bed.
Some people can't sleep but can't get up.
Four poster bed like a prison so you're
stuck.
The black tide rises. He'll drowned if he
doesn't recognize
It's not him. Not really.
The black blood works much better in
practice than in theory.

Most people bleed far more black than red.
We can't see it in their tears, you can't
see it in their sweat.
You can't see it in their eyes, you can't
see it in their heads.
Or maybe we can, maybe we just can't see
it yet.

- Shaun Kobrak

ANA
Once upon a time,
Long long ago,
I had a "friend" called Ana.
Who was no friend at all.
It look years to see her,
As the devil incarnate.
'Twas only on my death bed,
I realized she was no friend at all,
Rather a murdering bitch,
Whom I finally cast out of my mind,
In order that I might survive.

                    - Caroline Clancy

                    Poet_poetryofalifeinte
                    rrupted

ANA (2)
All I wanted was to be invisible,
I trusted Ana to help me,
But I didn't understand then,
That invisibility meant certain death.
I trusted Ana,
Blindly believing her wicked lies.
To the extent that we were One,
So deeply immersed were we,
That my life was no longer my own.
At deaths door I finally,
Recognized the truth of Ana,
That she'd never understood,
Me at all.

                    -   Caroline Clancy

                    Poet_poetryofalifeinterr
                    upted

On Monday my soul was full of stars and

brilliant things

On Tuesday nothing really had changed

On Wednesday things got all fucked up

On Thursday it took all my strength just to get

up

On Friday I tried to surrender,

I screamed, make it stop!

I just wanted my mind to remember, Monday I was

on top.

Now it's Saturday and things are okay

But I'm tired of having to take it day by day

On Sunday the week is over

I just want off this emotional rollercoaster

I feel so tired

So near the end

But I wrong, because

here comes Monday again.

                          -     anonymous

On the days that I feel like life
is too much
I know someone who's not sad
On the days that I feel like I'm not
enough
It can get really bad
I try to force a smile
But then I get mad
Because it's not easy
Those days when she comes out to play
There's nothing I can do to please me
I ask her to go away
But she drags me down
She chains me to my bed
It's so hard to get around
She is always three steps ahead

And if I manage to force her away
She reminds me that
Although she may be hidden
She's always up to chat
Although you can't see her
She's got this down to a T
Because I may hate to admit it
But she's a part of me
                    -   anonymous

Some days I am more prone to sadness.
For some unknown reason my defenses
are lowered and the air feels just
that little bit heavier.. that little
bit harder to breathe. But I know now,
that just like every other time, this
too shall pass. The air will become
light again and my lungs will welcome
each breath. Some people are just more
susceptible to sadness and the next
time this inevitably happens, I will
fight time through that 24 hours as
well. And I will continue to win.

                    - Annabelle Nunnery
                      Anopen_letter

Silence

Bipolar brain overthinking,
Like a never ending speed car,
Never stopping, never slowing.
I love the sound of silence,
To read a book to become,
So utterly absorbed,
That in that silence,
My mind is occupied by imaginative
narratives,
And nothing more.
My greatest relief.

                    - Caroline Clancy
                    Poet_poetryofalifeinterr
                    upted

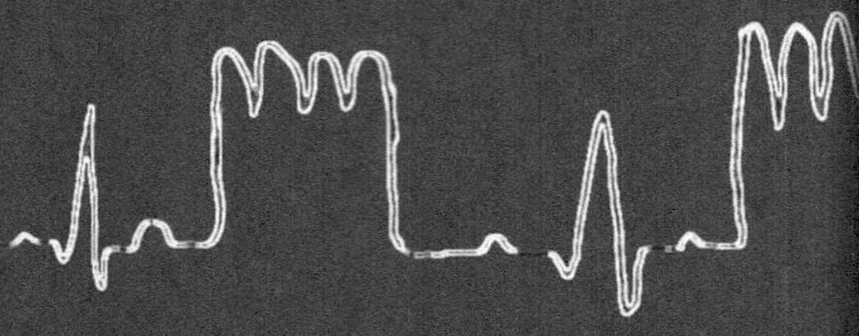

Some carry the world,
While others watch them carry until they
get old,
Some laugh out loud until they cry,
While others watch them with a wishful
sigh,
Some stand strong until they are broken,
While others are broken until being strong
is the only solution...

                    -   Najma Rai

                    The.travelingpoet

I wish I could shed my feelings like we shed

our clothes

Finding new in what used to be old

Searching for warmth after the cold

Wouldn't it be easy if we actually wore our

heart on our sleeves?

Just imagine what we could be

No more fatigue

No more anxiety

All in one swift move

Torn and reborn

into something new

We were all created together in harmony

Who am I to judge you?

Who are you to judge me?

                    -    anonymous

An apple for breakfast,
Some water for lunch,
When you get home,
Do not munch.

Food is bad
Water's your friend,
Now you know,
You must starve to the end.

- Kara Elia

Society simply says

 "cheer up!"

They don't think twice

I say I'm struggling

I expect them to do what's right

I'm full of confusing things

I just want them to help me fight

- anonymous

It was a black dog, all bites and no
barks,
A shadow so great that it swallowed my
spark.
Every day was a night that consumed
me,
It was a world with distorted edges,
Faces so blurred that I could not see.
That dog was so invisible, intangible,
all consuming - I was lost,
I was not the person in the mirror,
not a reflection but a ghost.
I was not numb, not desensitized, but
all consumed and full,
Full of absorption of the world's
problems so much I couldn't treat
treat my own
I felt worthless, voiceless,
purposeless, until I let myself
believe
And the way that other people loved me
was a way that I could feel.
That feeling breathed hope and that
hope breathed light,
And that black dog retreated, regained
my sight.
I saw love and hope and promise in the
person I could be,
And that black dog will retreat for
you if you will just
believe.

- Sarah McManus

On one fateful day,
It seems,
the worst of thoughts,
haunts my dreams.

And day by day,
the thoughts grow loud,
until it seems,
it's made a crowd.

The noise up there,
struts through my head,
causing most painful,
tears to shed.

And all it seems,
that I can do,
is cry and soak,
my pillows through,

Once my head,
is void of pain,
I heed the warnings,
From in my brain,

and now in conflict,
it seems I'll be,
for the rest,
of my eternity.

                    - Kara Elia

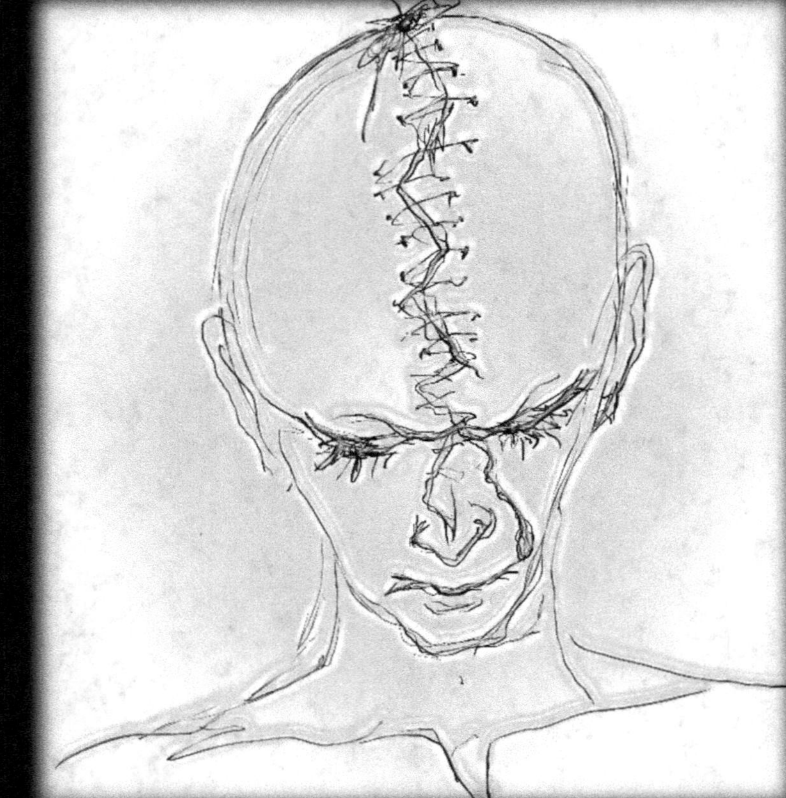

11,12,13,14,15,16,17

We're moving? Why? Who said we had
to? What will happen to my cats?

Well this place isn't so bad. What's
Mom doing? Why does she have a gun?
Why would she want him back
anyway?!...All those women….

Why is he here? Who is he? Oh look, a
puppy!   He's moving in?
Why am I locked out? Oh well, I can't
eat that. I don't have time. I need to
pick Mom up at work, go to church, pay
the light bill, and go get cheese at
the Government Office.

Where is our car? Did someone take it?
How will get to school? Did he burn my
clothes? Wait, is that him drunk and
asleep in the front seat of the car in
the garage? Pills/Vodka everywhere-
under the couch cushion, in the
medicine cabinet. He broke Mom's
necklace when he grabbed her! I look
better at 93 lbs. Is my hair falling
out? Why do I not have a period like
everyone else? Someone has got to get
him out of our house!

Who is the new guy? Why is bothering
me? You're marrying him? I'm moving
out? Can I take my cat? I look
better at 83 lbs. for sure.

Why is Dad not waving at me? Is he mad
or ashamed? Did he see me? ...Don't go
into the lunchroom. Everyone is in
there and they think I'm weird. I
don't need anything anyway. I gotta
get out of here.

                    -   anonymous

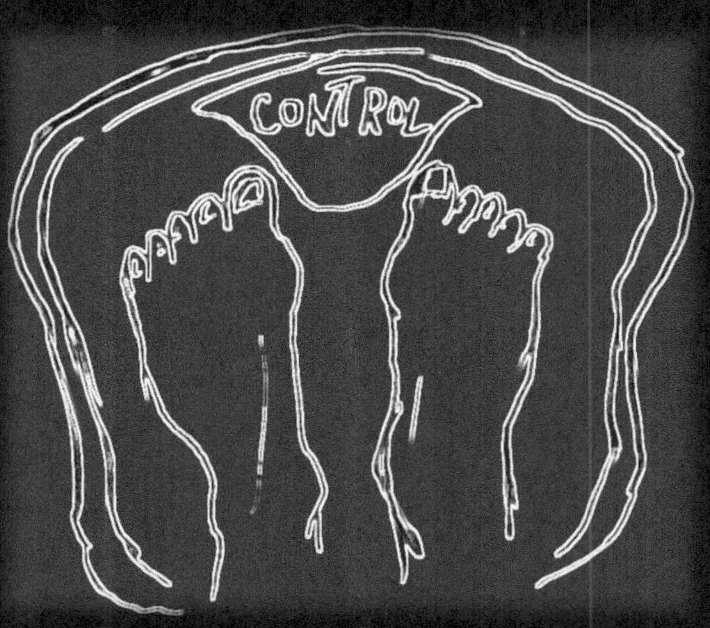

CONTROL

The Thrill

High as can be
But don't ask me

What you can't see
Is this is a part of me

It's the disease
It runs me

This isn't fun
To run and run

Until sun
Striving to feel some
But I feel none

The Stay

This has never happened before
Where's the door

Where's the mirror
Why can't someone make this clearer

You are More

You are

More than the words that broke you
More than the tears you shed

More than the pain they put you
through
More than the scars you created
You are more than this label

When Nightfall Hits

When nightfall hits
I call it quits
The pain sits

The tears fall
I've built a wall
Above it all

Somebody to Love Me

I just want
Someone to love me
To see me beyond the wall
To hear me when I don't call

To lean on when night falls
To love me when I forget to love
myself
Especially in times when I need help

Daytime Darkness

It's 2 pm
But the darkness clouds
There's no way out
These thoughts captivate me

I'm held in
A prisoner to a war
A war between myself

To live or die
To give it another try

To fight the hardest fight
The fight within me
The battle you can't see

What You Can't See

What you can't see is what he did to
me
The marks he left on me
The fear he instilled in me
The pain he inflicted upon me
Baby, I love you
Daddy, please stop

What you can't see is how I let her
down
How everyday she was ashamed of me
How often I was told I wasn't enough
Not smart enough
Not skinny enough
Not sweet enough
Not sane enough

What you can't see is how she wishes
I was normal
A healthy, pretty girl

Who loved herself
Who loved others
Who trusted others

What you can't see is that his image
is forever etched into my brain
Like a tattoo
One time sweet girl
The pain won't last forever
One night
Bruised, beaten, bleeding
Horrific screams

What you can't see
Is that I want to be happy
So bad
So bad it hurts

                  - anonymous

Braedon Bell is a college student
hoping to be an advocate for those who
lack a voice to speak on their own —
the voice of those who feel lost and
unworthy of recovery. She refuses to
stop until there is change. She is
hopeful the future will bring change
and proud to be a part of the mental
health campaign.

@mentalhealthcampaign_

www.ingramcontent.com/pod-product-compliance
Lightning Source LLC
Chambersburg PA
CBHW061512250726
48657CB00005B/1828